M000016840

Presented To:

....

From:

....

Date:

....

threadbare prayer

prayers for hearts
that feel hidden,
hurt, or hopeless

Stacey Thacker

Abingdon Press®
Growing in Life, Serving in Faith

NASHVILLE

THREADBARE PRAYER
PRAYERS FOR HEARTS THAT FEEL HIDDEN, HURT, OR HOPELESS

Copyright © 2020 Stacey Thacker
All rights reserved.

No part of this work may be reproduced or transmitted in any form or by any means, electronic or mechanical, including photocopying and recording, or by any information storage or retrieval system, except as may be expressly permitted by the 1976 Copyright Act or in writing from the publisher. Requests for permission can be addressed to Permissions, The United Methodist Publishing House, 2222 Rosa L. Parks Blvd., Nashville, TN 37228-1306 or emailed to permissions@umpublishing.org.

ISBN 978-1-7910-0801-7

Unless noted otherwise, Scripture quotations are from the ESV® Bible (The Holy Bible, English Standard Version®), copyright © 2001 by Crossway, a publishing ministry of Good News Publishers. Used by permission. All rights reserved.

Scripture quotations marked (NIV) are taken from the Holy Bible, New International Version®, NIV®. Copyright © 1973, 1978, 1984, 2011 by Biblica, Inc.™ Used by permission of Zondervan. All rights reserved worldwide. www.zondervan.com The "NIV" and "New International Version" are trademarks registered in the United States Patent and Trademark Office by Biblica, Inc.™

Scripture quotations noted (Voice) are taken from The Voice™. Copyright © 2008 by Ecclesia Bible Society. Used by permission. All rights reserved.

Scripture quotations noted (JBP) are taken from The New Testament in Modern English by J. B. Phillips copyright © 1960, 1972 J. B. Phillips. Administered by The Archbishops' Council of the Church of England. Used by Permission.

Scripture quotations marked NLT are taken from the Holy Bible, New Living Translation, copyright ©1996, 2004, 2015 by Tyndale House Foundation. Used by permission of Tyndale House Publishers, Inc., Carol Stream, Illinois 60188. All rights reserved.

Scripture quotations noted (NKJV) are taken from the New King James Version®. Copyright © 1982 by Thomas Nelson. Used by permission. All rights reserved.

Scripture quotations marked (GNT) are from the Good News Translation in Today's English Version- Second Edition © 1992 by American Bible Society. Used by Permission.

Published in association with the Books & Such Literary Agency, 52 Mission Circle, Suite 122, PMB 170, Santa Rosa, CA 95409-5370, www.booksandsuch.com.

Antique rug image used on cover and throughout book is courtesy of istock/combomambo.
Heart image used throughout book is courtesy of istock/leonardodesign21.
Thread image used throughout book is courtesy of Shutterstock/Rolling Orange.
Cover and interior design by Aesthetic Soup.

20 21 22 23 24 25 26 27 28 29 — 10 9 8 7 6 5 4 3 2 1
MANUFACTURED IN THE PEOPLE'S REPUBLIC OF CHINA

Dedication:

IU Cru Girls
Lisa, Robin, Stephanie, Unchong,
Tricia, Judy, and Samantha

I hold each of you in my heart.

"I thank my God in all my remembrance of you, always
in every prayer of mine for you all making my prayer
with joy, because of your partnership in the gospel from
the first day until now. And I am sure of this, that he
who began a good work in you will bring it to completion
at the day of Jesus Christ. It is right for me to feel this
way about you all, because I hold you in my heart...."

PHILIPPIANS 1:3-7A

Introduction

I propped my feet on the ottoman and noticed my jeans had finally worn thin enough at the knee to be considered stylish.

Threadbare they are.

I picked at the string still holding on for dear life and thought, how appropriate. I'm feeling every bit threadbare myself.

My nap is worn off.

Worn to the naked thread.

I'm hanging on for dear life.

I closed my eyes and remembered the day I bought these jeans about two years ago. *I was threadbare that day too.*

My husband was in the ICU after suffering a sudden cardiac arrest. Cardiac death they called it. He lingered in a coma for over a week but much to the surprise of everyone had awakened a couple of days before. We spent the better part of those few days retelling him the story of what had happened, meeting with doctors, and making plans for what came next.

On this particular day, the Tuesday following, I was torn in two. I needed to be with him bedside, but also at a different hospital in town with our 10-year-old daughter. She had a treatment scheduled that day. Her illness had reared its ugly head in the days before her daddy landed in his own hospital bed. We could not postpone and I needed to be the one to take her.

And so, I stretched thin and took her.

I left Mike across town with dear friends who promised to stand in for me. Between my daughter's pre-treatment doctor's appointment and her hospital visit, we ran into my favorite clothing store and bought these jeans. A little bit of normal in a truly hard day.

My big brother had sent me a gift card saying, *"This is for you to do something nice for yourself, sis. Don't you dare spend it on groceries. Get something for you."* I picked out a much-needed pair of jeans and a long pink cardigan. While waiting to check out, I alternately stuffed down my weariness and amusement for letting him boss me around again after so many years.

Finally, we settled in for her treatment, and as the day progressed, I received updates from Mike's ICU nurses and friends. I did my best to be present with my daughter. This was the first time ever after a year's worth of IV sticks she didn't cry. *"I'm not going to cry today, Mommy. I'm going to be brave like daddy."* And she was.

Around the four-hour mark of her treatment the other hospital called me. *"We need to transfer your husband to a different hospital immediately. You need to come and sign the papers."*

That would be the third hospital in my story.

I assured them I would be there as soon as I could, but heaven help us my daughter was still in her own hospital bed. They would have to wait for me and my signature.

I made it to my husband's ICU room around dinnertime and met with his doctors, who were adamant he needed to have surgery early the next morning at the other hospital.

I signed the paper.

I assured him that he was going to be OK. *(He doubted me.)*

I snuck my 10-year-old into the ICU so she could kiss her daddy. *(That helped.)*

And I watched as they wheeled him out the door.

I drove my exhausted brave girl home and sat down to a late dinner with my mom, who was taking care of my other three girls. I looked at her and said, *"I need to go to the new hospital and check on Mike."*

My mom folded her arms and said, *"Absolutely not. You*

need to go to bed. Call the nurse. Make sure he is settled, and tell them you will be there tomorrow for surgery bright and early." I resisted but only a little.

Threadbare doesn't have much pushback.

When I think on that Tuesday, I don't just remember it. I re-live it. My entire body feels the weight of it. I can see the hollow look in my eyes and the way I had to keep searching for a chair to sit down on because I was too exhausted to stand up.

But, looking back also reminds me that today's hard has been filtered through my shepherd's hands. The same ONE that walked me through that unbelievable ordeal two years ago is with me today.

When I don't have answers.

When my daughter is still sick.

When my husband struggles this side of a miracle.

When I see a mountain in front of me.

When suffering is long.

And I realize once again, Jesus isn't threadbare holding on for dear life.

He is holding on to me.

And he is before all things, and in him all things hold together. (Colossians 1:17).

Thredbare

THRED'BARE, *adjective* [thread and bare.]
Worn to the naked thread; having the nap worn
off; as a threadbare coat; threadbare clothes. [1]

---

1 S.V. Thredbare, Webster's Dictionary of 1828, http://webstersdictionary
1828.com/Dictionary/Thredbare, 03/28/2019.

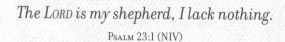

The L<small>ORD</small> is my shepherd, I lack nothing.
P<small>SALM</small> 23:1 (NIV)

Lord,

I'm so tired. I have nothing to offer. Yet, I am Martha worked up in the kitchen with a fear that you will look in and see me and think, *"Wow. She is not doing her part."*

When really, the problem is I'm trying to do all the parts.

God, I want to lean into you. I know you made me responsible for a reason. But is it keeping me from experiencing the peace and provision you have for me? I need your touch, Lord—and I need to see my tender and strong LACKING-NOTHING shepherd coming for me and holding me.

I am:
    vulnerable
      needy
        completely dependent on you

You:
    Are strong
      Have provision
        Have a table set up of abundance for me

Oh Lord, do what you can do. Show me today how you have gone before me and carved out paths of righteousness for me to follow. I need to see you today.

threadbare prayer:

LORD, you are my shepherd and I lack nothing.

"Since God cares for you,
let Him carry all your burdens and worries."

1 Peter 5:7 (Voice)

Lord,

Letting you carry some of my burdens and a few of my worries is ok.

But all, Lord?

They are many. They are heavy. And they are slowly draining the threadbare life right out of me. And so, as an act of faith I humble myself because I can't carry these anymore. I put the full weight on you:

My burdens:
finances
    healing
        leading well while broken

You are:
Abundant
    Strong
        In control

Lord, I come. Your strong hand has brought me here. I trust you to lift me up in your OWN good time. I'm putting the full weight of my anxieties on you and taking you at your WORD. _For I am your personal concern._ (See 1 Peter 5:6-7, JBP.)

threadbare prayer:

LORD, I will let you carry all my burdens and worries.

The LORD is good,
a stronghold in the day of trouble;
he knows those who take refuge in him.

NAHUM 1:7

Lord,

You are a good stronghold and I will take refuge in you today. When troubles surround me, I know I have a safe place to hide.

I am:
known
strengthened
held

You are:
The existing one—Jehovah
good and kind (I declare it even when I don't feel it)
a fortified place (when I can't hold myself up in a day of stress)

You know with certainty my heart, my thoughts, the way I take, the places I've been, and each fear I battle. And yet, you invite me to take refuge under the shadow of your sufficiency.

threadbare prayer:

LORD, only you know and that is enough for me.

> *"He found him in a desert land,
> and in the howling waste of the wilderness;
> he encircled him, he cared for him,
> he kept him as the apple of his eye."*
>
> DEUTERONOMY 32:10

Lord,

This certainly feels like a howling waste of the wilderness. It feels like I'm drowning on dry land. But you are not unfamiliar with finding your children in difficult places. This is where you found Jacob. It is where you found Hagar. And is where you find me, too. I'm so grateful you show up in unexpected places.

I am:
>seen
>>not alone
>>>cared for deeply and personally

You:
>Know where I am. Always
>>Wrap me up in all that you are
>>>Protect and care for me

What you have done for any of your children, at any time, you are able to do for me. Because YOU never change. You are the same ONE who encircles me, too.

threadbare prayer:

LORD, encircle me.

"…For we are powerless against this great horde that is coming against us. We do not know what to do, but our eyes are on you."

2 Chronicles 20:12

Lord,

My circumstances are not what I want them to be. There are situations outside my control. Right now, it feels as though I am facing the sea and an enemy is coming against me. *I have nowhere left to hide.*

But when I don't know what to do—I will look up. I will fix my eyes on you. I will position myself to see you and hear from your Word.

I am:
  unsure
    powerless
      surrounded

You are:
  All knowing
    Able to deliver
      Steady

There is a way. I just can't see it. There is a plan. You simply haven't revealed it. Yet. You are asking me to look to you.

threadbare prayer:

LORD, I don't know what to do, but my eyes are on you.

"and what is the immeasurable greatness of his power toward us who believe, according to the working of his great might that he worked in Christ when he raised him from the dead and seated him at his right hand in the heavenly places"

EPHESIANS 1:19-20

Lord,

Sometimes my memory is short. I forget who you are and the endless strength you possess. I forget that as your child, that same divine power lives inside of me, too. Your power doesn't simply make me able to stand, it causes dead things to come back to life.

I am:
    absent minded
      ineffective
        weak

You are:
    Thoughtful
      All powerful
        Fully alive

    Remind me today that your unlimited power is available to my weary heart. I don't have to produce it on my own; you provide it in abundance, causing me to come alive, too. I don't have a position of weakness; I have a place of power, strength, and victory.

threadbare prayer:

LORD, the same power that raised Christ lives in me.

"For the weapons of our warfare are not of the flesh but have divine power to destroy strongholds. We destroy arguments and every lofty opinion raised against the knowledge of God, and take every thought captive to obey Christ."

2 CORINTHIANS 10: 4-5

Lord,

It is easy when I'm hurting to believe untruths about who I am. I am asking you to unveil the lies I'm struggling with today. One by one, point your sword of truth so that I can clearly see them.

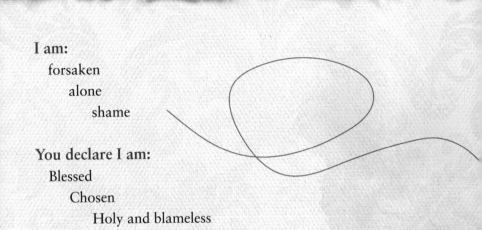

I am:
    forsaken
        alone
            shame

You declare I am:
    Blessed
        Chosen
            Holy and blameless

By the power of your Word, untangle every lie that sets itself as a stronghold in my heart. As you reveal them to me, I will take every thought and feeling and carry them to the foot of the cross—where you died to set me free. May I live to the praise of your glorious grace.

threadbare prayer:

LORD, unveil the lies I'm believing with your truth.

Because he bends down to listen,
I will pray as long as I have breath!

Psalm 116:2 (NLT)

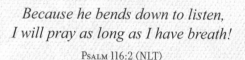

Lord,

You pay attention to the faintest of prayers from the most desperate hearts. You hear my cry for help whether it is early in the morning or in the middle of the day. Not only do you hear, but you stoop down to listen, as if I was a little child, not wanting to miss a single word spoken.

I am:
whispering prayers
distressed
sorrowful

You are:
Personal
Listening
Merciful to answer

Your commitment to bend down low to constantly listen to my heart gives me peace. It makes me love to pray. You are poised and positioned to hear my plea for help—even when all I can breathe out is, "Jesus." You hear and you answer.

threadbare prayer:

LORD, I will breathe out constant prayers, because you are listening.

Likewise the Spirit helps us in our weakness. For we do not know what to pray for as we ought, but the Spirit himself intercedes for us with groanings too deep for words.

ROMANS 8:26

Lord,

In my weakness you draw me close and pray for me. Your Holy Spirit passes between me and the Father praying perfectly for His Will. My words aren't even necessary because you know my heart deeply.

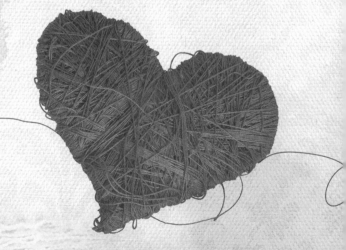

I don't know:
>> what I need
>>>> how to pray
>>>>>> the right timing

You know:
>> My weakness
>>>> The words to say
>>>>>> When to answer

There is freedom and comfort in knowing that if I can't call up the words, you are not speechless. This constant prayer conversation is continual and filled with hope. We are all hoping, Lord.

threadbare prayer:

LORD, I don't know what to pray, but you do.

And Hannah prayed and said,
"My heart exults in the LORD;
my horn is exalted in the LORD.
My mouth derides my enemies,
because I rejoice in your salvation.
"There is none holy like the LORD:
for there is none besides you;
there is no rock like our God."

1 SAMUEL 2:1-2

Lord,

You are good. I know it deep down in my heart. But today, I don't really want to pray. I feel like a broken record bringing the same petition before you. So, I'm here, by faith, to lean into your strength.

I am:
   barren
      bruised
         broken

You are:
   Holy
      A refuge
         My strength

   I am opening my heart to you
once again because I have learned over and
over again, the best place to be found is in your
presence. As I'm waiting for you to answer, you are building
my faith and making me strong, and I will praise you for it.

threadbare prayer:

LORD, my strength rises in your holy presence.

Praise the Lord; praise God our savior!
For each day he carries us in his arms.

PSALM 68:19 (NLT)

Lord,

Life is so daily. In the midst of all that comes against me, remind me that your power and promises persist as well.

I am:
    striving
        needy
            battle weary

You are:
    Triumphant
        Sufficient
            Good

When I need shelter, you cover me. When I need daily bread, you rain it down from heaven. If I need a defender. you come quickly to protect me. It doesn't matter what I need, you can provide it. It is amazing to me that you do all of this while tenderly carrying me in your arms. Focusing on your daily care of me brings me such comfort because nobody cares for me like this but you, Jesus.

threadbare prayer:

LORD, I praise you because you carry me every day.

Show me grace, Eternal God. I am completely undone.
Bring me back together, Eternal One. Mend my shattered bones.

PSALM 6:2 (VOICE)

Lord,

From morning to night. I pour out simple prayers to you.
I don't have any fine or fancy words to string together.
This is only me, humbly telling you what is in my heart.

I am:
    undone
        weeping
            beyond exhaustion

You are:
    Welcoming
        Filled with compassion
            Steadfast

Yet in my brokenness I come to you confident that in your ears, my prayers are more than mere words. You hear my cry for help and put me back together. In your kindness you show me grace because you not only move on my behalf, you move me towards wholeness and healing.

threadbare prayer:

LORD, show me grace.

> *"Come to me, all who labor and are heavy laden,
> and I will give you rest."*
>
> MATTHEW 11:28

Lord,

I'm busy and worn out. The weariness I am experiencing at times feels like dead weight upon my entire being. You have been calling my name over and over, but in my frenzied state I have ignored you. I'm sorry. I need you, Lord, more than my words express. Your invitation is clear, "Come to me."

I am:
carrying too much
anxious
bothered

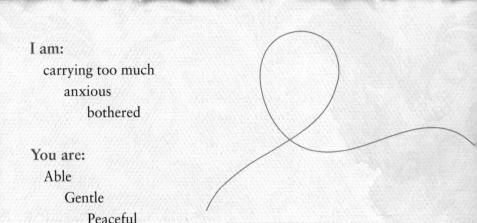

You are:
Able
Gentle
Peaceful

I want to drink in the quietness of your presence like living water to my thirsty soul. It feels so foreign to the way I live. Thank you for your promise to stay with me and show me how to take real rest. I'm holding onto this promise in particular and praying it back to you as an act of faith. I know you will answer and honor your Word.

threadbare prayer:

LORD, show me how to take a real rest.

"There is no fear in love, but perfect love casts out fear.
For fear has to do with punishment,
and whoever fears has not been perfected in love."

1 JOHN 4:18

Lord,

Lately, I have lost sight of the freedom your love brings to my life. I have looked sideways at my sister instead of up and only to you. I have coveted what she holds in her hands. I have wanted it for myself. Comparison doesn't have one ounce of love in it and comes from a place of fear, so I want to leave it far behind today.

I am:
    fearful
        jealous
            prideful

You are:
    Loving
        Selfless
            Perfect

I'm wooed by the thought of your relentless love for me. It simply never stops. You are not impressed by me, either. There is freedom in that type of love when I let it sink down to the very depths of my soul. I don't need what my sister has because your perfect love supplies all I need forever.

threadbare prayer:

LORD, let your well-formed love be in me.

Sing to the LORD a new song,
his praise from the end of the earth,
you who go down to the sea, and all that fills it,
the coastlands and their inhabitants.

ISAIAH 42:10

Lord,

Sometimes I let fear bury my song. Fear doesn't want me to praise you. Fear wants me to collapse inside myself and worry. I have been silent long enough. Today I will sing.

I will:
    raise my voice
        sing for joy
            give you all the glory

You will:
    Take hold of my hand
        Keep me
            Do a new thing

I'm choosing to let my worship rise up and declare your goodness, despite my circumstances, saying, "God will provide. He will not abandon me. He is good." This is my song of absolute trust in You. My hope is that when others hear me singing they will join me in the chorus of praising your holy name.

threadbare prayer:

LORD, I will sing a new song.

"Ah, Lord GOD! It is you who have made the heavens and the earth by your great power and by your outstretched arm! Nothing is too hard for you."

JEREMIAH 32:17

Lord,

On my most difficult days, I find sweet freedom in pouring out my heart to you. You welcome my lament, entreating me to unburden my heart and hold nothing back.

I am:
unformed
brokenhearted
limited

You are:
Creator
Sustainer
Extraordinary

Free of my fears and frustrations, I can clearly see that my problems do not cause you stress in the least. Instead, you gently dry my tears and point to the stars saying, "Look at my handiwork. Do you think anything is too hard for me?" In that moment of adoration, I find my soul resting upon your glory and goodness.

threadbare prayer:
LORD, nothing is too hard for you.

So she called the name of the LORD who spoke to her,
"You are a God of seeing," for she said,
"Truly here I have seen him who looks after me."

GENESIS 16:13

Lord,

There are days when I want to run away and hide from the pressing needs around me. And yet, if I'm honest, I also want to run to be seen. I wonder if anyone would notice if I closed the bathroom door and stayed there for an hour or two. Would they come looking for me because they care or because I am useful to them? This battle continues until I find myself rightly running towards you—the One who Sees me.

I am:
    hiding
        longing to be found
            conflicted

You:
    See me
        Meet me in my hiding place
            Take care of me

El Roi is your name. The God who sees—sees me. I can lean into your name and find such comfort in knowing that my longing to run can lead me right to you. You see. You care. You seek my heart and send me back with the assurance that I am never unfound. I am safe in the compassionate care of your all-seeing heart.

threadbare prayer:

LORD, you see me.

For I am convinced that neither death nor life, neither angels nor demons, neither the present nor the future, nor any powers, neither height nor depth, nor anything else in all creation, will be able to separate us from the love of God that is in Christ Jesus our Lord.

Romans 8:38-39 (NIV)

Lord,

You love me in the most extraordinary way, and I'm never left to wonder "What if?" You've settled that already through the cross by stretching out your arms and saying, "This is how much I love you."

I know that:
   no anxiety
      no pain
         nothing at all or anywhere can disconnect me
         from your love

You:
   Found me
      Fought death and won
         Freed me

Living with this kind of love as the undercurrent of my life truly changes everything. My heart is secure knowing it doesn't matter what I'm faced with today. I can't be separated from your love by anything above the earth or on the earth. I have your promise. Your love does not fail.

threadbare prayer:

LORD, your strong love does not fail.

But you, O Lord, are a shield about me,
my glory, and the lifter of my head.

Psalm 3:3

Lord,

It isn't like the first sign of trials sent me headlong into a pit. But the third, fourth, and fifth round has greatly discouraged me. Still, I find deep encouragement in knowing that when I come to the end of myself—you are not exhausted. Instead,

I can face:
the enemy
my fears
any trial that comes my way

You:
Wrap me up
Provide an abundance in your presence
Lift my eyes upward

I know on my worst days, in the fiercest battle, I can cry out to you. Your answer comes as an embrace and sets me in the safest place possible. I can rest easy knowing that the battle belongs to you while I'm surrounded by your glory.

threadbare prayer:

LORD, you wrap me up, safe.

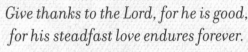

Give thanks to the Lord, for he is good,
for his steadfast love endures forever.

PSALM 136:1

Lord,

It is good for me to think back to all that you have done for me. When I make this mental list, your kindness does not let me stay discouraged for long. You remind me that gratitude has the power of turning my problems into a reason to always praise you.

I am:
    quick to forget
        looking for deliverance
            seeking the courage to take the next step

You are:
    Sufficiently kind
        The One who split the sea
            Giver of all I need

In order to stop the descent of my discontent, I need to recall not just what you have done but also who you are. There is always a reason to praise you. I will choose to bless you and see your kindness coming again and again, like waves on the shore, to rescue my heart from discouragement and defeat.

threadbare prayer:

LORD, your kindness does not quit.

"Behold, I am doing a new thing;
now it springs forth, do you not perceive it?
I will make a way in the wilderness
and rivers in the desert."

ISAIAH 43:19

Lord,

I'm not sure how I came to be in this hard place yet
again. This wilderness has become familiar to me. so I
know you are here with me. Even though I can't see from
my vantage point the purpose in this path, I will
keep in mind:

I am:
    your daughter
        created for your glory
            redeemed for a reason

You are:
    Leading me
        Doing a new thing
            Making a way in the wilderness

When my back is against the wall, the path appears to be blocked, and my enemy is threatening to destroy me, I will trust the way you are making. You always do. You always have. I believe in the end the way you've made will lead me to greater depths with you and your greatest glory.

threadbare prayer:

LORD, you are making a way.

*"And there I will give her her vineyards
and make the Valley of Achor a door of hope.
And there she shall answer as in the days of her youth,
as at the time when she came out of the land of Egypt."*

HOSEA 2:15

Lord,

I realize you sometimes lead me into difficult places so that I can experience your presence in a much richer way. It is here, when the noise of the world has quieted, that I actually hear you more clearly. In the valley of my deepest soul ache, you promise to turn my troubles into a doorway that is filled with hope.

I am:
  troubled
    grieving
      silent

You:
  Take me to the wilderness
    Speak to my heart
      Show me the door of hope

You meet me here and never leave me alone to break to pieces. You stay. You sing softly. And when my heart is ready, you give me your song to sing too.

threadbare prayer:

LORD, you turn my troubles into a door of hope.

For you are all children of light, children of the day.
We are not of the night or of the darkness.

1 Thessalonians 5:5

Lord,

You are the light of the world. As your daughter, I am filled with your light-bearing Spirit as well. Even when the darkness seems to press in all around me, I can choose to reflect your light.

I will:
    walk in the light of your truth.
        shine bright for you, daily.
            resist the darkness

You:
    Are the source of the light
        Have the power to dispel the darkness
            Light my path as I take steps of faith

The world is veiled in darkness, but in you there is no darkness at all. I will remember today that as your daughter I bear your image and carry your light to a lost and dying world. There is no night that is so dark that the daylight can't shatter it.

threadbare prayer:

LORD, remind me I am a daughter of the day.

*And I looked and arose and said to the nobles
and to the officials and to the rest of the people,
"Do not be afraid of them. Remember the Lord,
who is great and awesome, and fight for your brothers,
your sons, your daughters, your wives, and your homes."*

NEHEMIAH 4:14

Lord,

There are days when I set out to do what you have
asked me to do and I find an army of opposition trying to
discourage me and distract me from your plan. Sometimes
I have to physically stop what I'm doing and say aloud,
"My God is greater than the company
that is coming against me."
Because you are.

I will:
    not let fear dictate my duty
        focus my attention on you
            remember who you are

You are:
    Great
        Awesome
            In control of the outcome

So today I will get up, I will do the work you have called me to do, and I will set my gaze steadily on your greatness. I will shut out the noise from those around me who want to frustrate my work unto you. I will keep to the task knowing you can handle whatever comes my way.

threadbare prayer:

LORD, I will remember you are GREAT and AWESOME.

Therefore, my beloved brothers, be steadfast,
immovable, always abounding in the work of the Lord,
knowing that in the Lord your labor is not in vain.

1 Corinthians 15:58

Lord,

The Gospel has true power over my heart. There is nothing more encouraging to give me strength to stand. I need to preach it to myself every single day until I believe it.

I will:
be steadfast
stand unshakable
work with all my heart

Because You:
Defeated my greatest enemy
Denied his stronghold over me
Declared there is no more sting from death

Being steadfast means I will not quit. I will endure. The reason I can is because sin has no power, guilt has no shame, and death has no hold over me. You defeated them at the cross. And on that I will stand.

threadbare prayer:

LORD, in you I will stand steadfast.

"The LORD will fight for you, and you have only to be silent." The LORD said to Moses, "Why do you cry to me? Tell the people of Israel to go forward. Lift up your staff, and stretch out your hand over the sea and divide it, that the people of Israel may go through the sea on dry ground."

EXODUS 14:14-16

Lord,

My perspective and yours are often very different. I see a wilderness place as failure. I see my enemies overtaking me, I feel hedged in on all sides, and it looks to me like there is no way out. But the truth is, you are the God who works wonders as I take steps of quiet faith.

I will:
    stop complaining
        listen for your instruction
           calmly step forward

You will:
    Surround me
        Fight my battles
           Part the sea

You are not worried about the wilderness. In your Word you often set barren places as a backdrop for your ultimate rescue. Because you are unchanging, I will trust that you have drawn me here to quietly witness your glory on full display.

threadbare prayer:

LORD, you work wonders as I take quiet steps of faith.

You will keep in perfect peace,
those whose minds are steadfast,
because they trust in you.
Trust in the Lord forever,
for the Lord, the Lord himself, is the Rock eternal.

Isaiah 26:3-4 (NIV)

Lord,

You are a strong tower I can run to when life around me swirls out of control. This complete and constant peace is kept and guarded by you for me. I will keep my mind firmly fixed on you because you are an unmoving rock of stability.

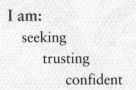

I am:
seeking
trusting
confident

You are:
Perfect peace
A fortress
Everlasting

In the midst of difficult chapters in my story that I would rather forget, may others look in astonishment and glorify your name—Jehovah Shalom. The Lord of peace, I will be found singing and trusting in you.

threadbare prayer:

LORD, you keep me in perfect peace.

Therefore confess your sins to each other and pray for each other so that you may be healed. The prayer of a righteous person is powerful and effective.

JAMES 5:16 (NIV)

Lord,

You tell me to come to you at all times with every need I have. I believe you invite me to pray because you are willing to open the gates of heaven on behalf of your children.

I will pray:
> with a clean heart
>> seeking a relationship with you
>>> fervently

You:
> Invite us to pray
>> Hear our prayers
>>> Enable our prayers

It is a blessing to take my mind off my own problems and passionately pray for others without stopping. Being persistent in prayer takes a clean heart and great faith. But I will remember that great faith releases great power.

threadbare prayer:

LORD, I will pray long and hard.

"For the eyes of the Lord run to and fro throughout the whole earth, to give strong support to those whose heart is blameless toward him."

2 Chronicles 16:9a

Lord,

In spite of my best intentions, I run out of my own strength pretty quickly. I can't always depend on those around me to notice I'm drowning in the middle of my life. But nothing goes unseen by you—not my weariness nor my frustration.

I am:
doing my best
wholly committed to you
desperate for encouragement

You:
Are more than enough
Eagerly search for me
Sustain and strengthen me

I've learned, where your eyes run, so does your strong support. It is unbelievable to me, and a constant source of sweet encouragement that you are constantly scanning your creation looking for your beloved children. It is a gift that your care is quick because I am never too far gone from your sustaining grace.

threadbare prayer:

LORD, you seek to strengthen.

"But seek first the kingdom of God and his righteousness, and all these things will be added to you. Therefore do not be anxious about tomorrow, for tomorrow will be anxious for itself. Sufficient for the day is its own trouble."

MATTHEW 6:33-34

Lord,

I admit that up until now, worry has been a way of life for me. I've let it interfere with my worship of who you are and what you are doing today.

I will:
worship first
be careless in your care
focus on what you are doing right now

You:
Know what I need
Provide faithfully
Help me face tomorrow when the time comes

Worry borrows trouble that may never come my way. It causes me to imagine I am responsible for everything on my own. Nothing could be further from the truth. I want to seek you today and acknowledge that you are already taking care of all that I need. At the same time, you are taking care of future things I don't need to concern myself with today.

threadbare prayer:

LORD, tomorrow is yours. I will not worry about it.

I knew he would speak
to my heart and, ultimately,
he was the door of hope
I could walk through.

The Wilderness

In 2014, my dad died suddenly of a pulmonary embolism after a long battle with cancer. I planned on a long goodbye, and instead received an abrupt departure. It was during that season I began to understand that Threadbare prayer happens in the wilderness. Since then, I've learned that nothing prepares you for the wilderness like spending time in the wilderness. My own threadbare wilderness preparation included walking through the wilderness of grief after losing my dad. I knew what the valley of the shadow of death felt like because I had walked through it before. During that time, God wrote a particular verse on my heart from the book of Hosea that says,

"Therefore, behold, I will allure her,
and bring her into the wilderness,

and speak tenderly to her.
And there I will give her her vineyards
and make the Valley of Achor a door of hope.
And there she shall answer as in the days of her youth,
as at the time when she came out of the land of Egypt."

(Hosea 2:14-15)

I knew from personal experience the wilderness was a place God was leading me to and through. It had a beginning, middle, and end. I knew he would speak to my heart and, ultimately, he was the door of hope I could walk through.

My wilderness was not limited to grieving my dad though. The year after he passed away, I walked through another wilderness of unknown outcomes during the hospitalization of my eight-year-old daughter. We spent days in the hospital trying to discover what was making her so sick. In the early moments of her mysterious illness, I was holding my breath until a doctor told me she was going to be OK. I honestly didn't know. In this wilderness I prayed simple prayers and wrestled hard with the Lord. I wanted to know why. I wanted to know how long. Mostly I wanted to know what God was going to do to fix my little girl.

During this wilderness I didn't have chapters of biblical truth flowing in and out of my heart. I simply wrestled and then held fast to Jesus knowing he could handle my hurt and he would work it out in his good time. My shepherd was not one bit surprised by this second trip inside a year back into the wilderness. Truthfully, I was still in the same wilderness, struggling with a continued sense of loss, fear, and helplessness. But Jesus had gone before me, calling my name and saying ever so gently, "I hold all things together. Even you" (see Hebrews 1:3). And he did.

Losing my dad and then receiving my daughter's diagnosis of a chronic illness were times of struggle and loss. But, in comparison to what I would face in later days with my husband, they were lesser difficulties through which God was laying foundations of trust and preparation for a much greater trial where my threadbare heart would be tested even more.

But now thus says the Lord,
he who created you, O Jacob,
he who formed you, O Israel:
"Fear not, for I have redeemed you;
I have called you by name, you are mine.
When you pass through the waters, I will be with you;
and through the rivers, they shall not overwhelm you;
when you walk through fire you shall not be burned,
and the flame shall not consume you."

Isaiah 43:1-2

Lord,

You have always paid special attention to your distressed
children. You do not abandon or cease to care
because your love is present and enduring.

When I:
    find myself afraid of everything
        face the fiercest storm
            walk through fire threatening to engulf me

You remind me that you:
    Shaped me
        Set me free
            Know my name

    You have not only named me, but you have claimed me as your own. You aren't about to leave me. It isn't a question of *if* I pass through the waters or face the fire of trials, but *when*. Therefore, I will take great comfort in your knowing presence and not let fear run off with my heart.

threadbare prayer:

LORD, you know my name. I will not be afraid.

> *"Have I not commanded you? Be strong and courageous.*
> *Do not be frightened, and do not be dismayed,*
> *for the LORD your God is with you wherever you go."*
>
> JOSHUA 1:9

Lord,

    You know where I've been and where I'm going. Over and over again your Word calls me to take courage and be brave. There is no place I have been or will ever go that you are not with me.

I will:
　　take you at your word
　　　　bravely step out
　　　　　　be careful to obey

You:
　　Are my God
　　　　You remain with me
　　　　　　You keep your promises

　　You have rescued me. You have redeemed me. You have carved out the path and spoken courage into my heart by the power of your Word. I will boldly take possession today of all you have promised.

threadbare prayer:
LORD, you are the reason I can be brave.

Bless the LORD, O my soul,
and all that is within me,
bless his holy name!
Bless the LORD, O my soul,
and forget not all his benefits,
who forgives all your iniquity,
who heals all your diseases,
who redeems your life from the pit,
who crowns you with steadfast love and mercy,
who satisfies you with good
so that your youth is renewed like the eagle's.

PSALM 103:1-5

Lord,

The enemy would prefer I focus
on my circumstances and complain.
The remedy is remembering there is
an abundance of reasons to stir up my
soul to pour out my praise to you.

I am:
  forgiven
      cured
          rescued

You:
  Lavishly crown me with love and mercy
      Give me the favor of your grace
          Renew me with new life every day

Blessing after blessing reminds me of the power of praise to pull me out of the pit of despair and lift my gaze to you. I won't ask for anything else today. You have healed me. You have forgiven me. You have crowned me with your loving-kindness. You have been so good to me. I will simply be satisfied with what you have given and praise you with my whole heart.

threadbare prayer:
LORD, I will bless you.

For because he himself has suffered when tempted,
he is able to help those who are being tempted.

HEBREWS 2:18

Lord,

I am awestruck with the thought that you entered into
humanity not only to save my soul, but also to help me in
my everyday struggles.

I am:
    being tested
        under continuous attack
            crying to you for help

You:
    Powerfully overcame every test
        Experienced suffering
            Come quickly to help me

As I fix my eyes on you, I see that you are Jehovah Ezer, which means The LORD My Help. Indeed, you run towards me, with deep compassion and skillful care. At the same time, because you lived a perfect, sin-free life, you have the power to help me overcome every temptation or trial that comes my way.

threadbare prayer:

LORD, you run to help me when I cry out.

*May the God of hope fill you with all joy
and peace in believing, so that by the power
of the Holy Spirit you may abound in hope.*

Romans 15:13

Lord,

I've never met one person who doesn't need hope,
myself included. Some days, it feels like hope is far off and
unattainable. But you are the author of hope and where I
need to turn when I need to be filled up.

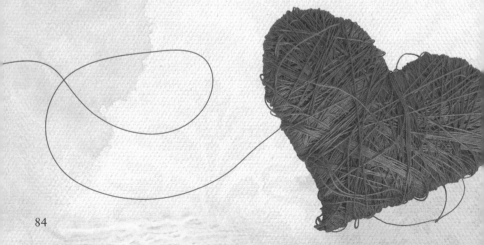

I am:
  burned out
    emptied
      melancholy

You:
  Author hope
    Bring joy and peace
      Pour out overflowing hope

I can shift my focus in this moment and remember that hope isn't your personality trait, hope is WHO you are. Your dynamic power ignites my heart not only with hope, but with joy and peace as well. This is the contagious hope I truly want in my life for others to see and experience as well. Oh Lord, let it be true today of me.

threadbare prayer:

LORD, you fill me with abounding hope.

So we do not lose heart. Though our outer self is wasting away, our inner self is being renewed day by day. For this light momentary affliction is preparing for us an eternal weight of glory beyond all comparison, as we look not to the things that are seen but to the things that are unseen. For the things that are seen are transient, but the things that are unseen are eternal.

2 CORINTHIANS 4:16-18

Lord,

There is more than meets the eye going on in my life. I look around me and it seems like everything is falling apart. But on closer examination I see what you are really doing. You are preparing me for glory and that takes a closer look.

I:
    see outward troubles
        sense you are doing more
            can choose my focus

You:
    Use my passing trials
        Restore my soul
            Create for me an eternal glory far beyond
            my imagination

I will not let discouragement cause me to despair because
you are always at work in unseen ways. At the same time,
my temporary troubles are light when I compare them to the
everlasting reward that will bring you glory forever.

threadbare prayer:

LORD, I will not lose heart because you are working where
it matters most.

"I am the Alpha and the Omega," says the Lord God,
"who is and who was and who is to come, the Almighty."

Lord,

Today I need to hear that it is going to be OK. I could message a friend, or post on social media and look for these words from someone else but that won't truly bring peace to my anxious heart. Instead, I need to open your Word and consider what you already said.

I am:
    worried about mistakes I've made
        wondering what to do today
            unsure about the long-term plan

You are:
    The beginning
        With me in the in-between
            The ending

The reason I don't need to be afraid is because you hold my is, my was, and my is to come in your gracious tender hands. There is nothing that has been or will be that you aren't sovereign over or making better. It is going to be OK because you make it OK.

threadbare prayer:

LORD, you have my was, is, and is to come.

And behold, there arose a great storm on the sea,
so that the boat was being swamped by the waves;
but he was asleep. And they went and woke him, saying,
"Save us, Lord; we are perishing." And he said to them,
"Why are you afraid, O you of little faith?" Then he rose
and rebuked the winds and the sea, and there was
a great calm. And the men marveled, saying, "What
sort of man is this, that even winds and sea obey him?"

MATTHEW 8:24-27

Lord,

There is nothing outside of your control. You have
divine authority over all things. Even when a sudden life-
threatening storm comes my way, I don't have to be afraid.

I:

    see the wind

        focus on the waves

            cry out to you

You:

    Hear me when I call

        You are not confused or worried

            Nothing takes you by surprise

My cry cuts through the roar of the storm right to your heart because you are near. In the moment when I'm sure my world is going to crumble, you turn chaos into calm waters. My faith is small, but you speak the word and even the winds and waves listen and obey because they recognize your voice.

threadbare prayer:

LORD, with a word, you calm the storm.

He who dwells in the shelter of the Most High
will abide in the shadow of the Almighty.
I will say to the LORD, "My refuge and my fortress,
my God, in whom I trust."

PSALM 91:1-2

Lord,

The shelter of the Most-High God is a secret place I can tuck myself into for safe keeping. You invite me to make this my home so I can be as close to you as I can get, while far away from the danger and fears that are coming against me.

I:
    dwell here
        stay and rest
            declare my trust in you

You:
    Provide a place near you
        Shelter
            Defend

I have a choice to make. I can let fear drive me to trying to take care of myself, or I can let it drive me to the safe shelter of your shadow. One will take everything I have, the other will give me all that you are—Almighty, LORD, Trustworthy—my God in whom I trust.

threadbare prayer:

LORD, you are my secret dwelling place.

And we know that all things work together
for good to those who love God.

ROMANS 8:28 (NKJV)

Lord,

You have plans for my life that I believe are for my good and your glory. I know that you know me better than I know myself, so I will look to you as you work it all out.

I:
love you
have a purpose-filled calling
trust your plan

You:
Care deeply for me
Orchestrate a plan for your glory
Are working towards something good for me

I know that everything in my life may not be a good thing in and of itself. But in your hands, you can bring good from it. I don't have to worry about every little thing because I know that you are faithful. I place myself in your capable hands to work out your good plan in my life.

threadbare prayer:

LORD, work for my good and your glory.

Immediately the father of the child cried out and said,
"I believe; help my unbelief!"

Mark 9:24

Lord,

I admit that my belief is thin right now. I BELIEVE in you and who you are, but sometimes I don't believe you are here, right now, and working in my current situation. I think you answer other people's prayers, just not mine.

I:
    cry out in desperation
        believe
            yet struggle to believe you in this

You:
    See me struggling
        Love me in spite of my weak faith
            Show me all things are possible

    The question has never been about your power to perform, but my willingness to place my weak faith in your hands. Even in the face of what seems impossible, you demonstrate all things are possible in you, through you, with you, when I believe.

threadbare prayer:

LORD, I believe, help me believe more.

In peace I will both lie down and sleep;
for you alone, O LORD, make me dwell in safety.

PSALM 4:8

Lord,

During the day, when I'm busy, I can push back my fears. But at night, they seem to torment my rest. I treasure this promise from your Word that reminds me otherwise.

I can:
    lie down
        sleep
            dwell in confident trust

You:
    Are peace
        Keep me safe
            Give me rest

The security found in you when I lie down and sleep is more than just a fact, it is a feeling. I can remember you are the same one who was able to sleep in the bow of the boat during a fierce storm, and I can do the same.

threadbare prayer:

LORD, I can lie down in peaceful sleep.

You hem me in, behind and before,
and lay your hand upon me.
Such knowledge is too wonderful for me;
it is high; I cannot attain it.

PSALM 139:5-6

Lord,

    I can look back and see you have never left me.
Wherever I am going, you are already there. At the same
time, I find myself in awe of your constant presence.
My mind can't grasp how you are always with me. It is
something of a mystery.

I am:
    never alone
        secure
            known

You go:
    Before me
        With me
            Behind me

You tenderly carry me like you would a precious treasure. Every place I turn I have evidence that I am enfolded in your embrace, forever and always.

threadbare prayer:

LORD, you go before me, with me, and follow behind me, always.

*"Finally, be strong in the Lord
and in the strength of his might."*

Ephesians 6:10

Lord,

Everyday life has pressed hard on me and I need your mighty strength today. My strength comes from you because I have been placed in Christ. Not only do you empower me, you have already won the battle.

I am:
> defenseless
>> limited
>>> drawing on your strength

You are:
> Boundless in power
>> Strengthening me
>>> Already victorious

Prayer is how I keep in constant connection to you—drawing not on my source of strength, but yours. I will direct my words to you today so I can resist the enemy, experience your powerful presence, and hold my ground.

threadbare prayer:

LORD, I will draw my strength from you.

But he answered, "It is written,
"'Man shall not live by bread alone,
but by every word that comes from the mouth of God.'"

MATTHEW 4:4

Lord,

My lonesome and hungry heart needs to be sustained with soul-filled words I find when I open the Bible and feast on the abundance at your table.

I:
   need your Word
        listen to your Word
              will daily feast on your Word alone

Your Word:
   Comforts
        Convicts me of sin
              Strengthens

   Your Word not only satisfies my deepest need but is also my protector. I know the enemy can't defeat a heart that is filled with the living, active, sharp Word of God.

threadbare prayer:

LORD, only your Word satisfies my hungry heart.

But they who wait for the LORD shall renew their strength;
they shall mount up with wings like eagles;
they shall run and not be weary;
they shall walk and not faint.

ISAIAH 40:31

Lord,

In my most threadbare moments, I am tempted to work harder and faster and keep moving at a frenzied pace in my own strength. But this isn't what you desire for me. You say, "Wait for me" and then expect me to do it.

I am:
weak
   weary
      fainthearted

You are:
Everlasting
   Tireless
      All powerful

You never get tired or worn thin. I marvel at this. When I remember that you see all, know all, and have endless power, I can pause and hope in you completely. In that moment, I find God-sized strength that never fails.

threadbare prayer:

LORD, I will wait for you.

Not only that, but we rejoice in our sufferings,
knowing that suffering produces endurance,
and endurance produces character, and character
produces hope, and hope does not put us to shame,
because God's love has been poured into our hearts
through the Holy Spirit who has been given to us.

ROMANS 5:3–5

Lord,

I can choose joy when I go through
troubled times because I know that
as I endure you are producing
something of great worth
in me.

I will grow in:
    endurance
        character
           hope

You promise:
    Not to put us to shame
        To pour out your love
           To give us the gift of the Holy Spirit

Hope allows our character to be tried, but it will not put us to shame or fail to satisfy our deepest need. Your abundant love overflowing in our lives is all the proof we need that the process is worth it.

threadbare prayer:

LORD, your hope-filled promises never disappoint me.

"Now the Lord is the Spirit, and where the Spirit of the Lord is, there is freedom. And we all, with unveiled face, beholding the glory of the Lord, are being transformed into the same image from one degree of glory to another. For this comes from the Lord who is the Spirit."

2 Corinthians 3:17-18

Lord,

Where you dwell, there is always freedom giving light. You are personal and present and no longer hidden behind the protective veil. I have access to you every single moment.

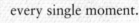

I:
    see you face-to-face
        am truly free
            reflect your glory more and more

You:
    Call me your friend
        Live within me
            Transform me day by day

In the light and liberty of the Gospel I turn to you and there is nothing between us because you have made your home in my heart. Face-to-face I can see your glory and it changes me completely.

threadbare prayer:

LORD, freedom means seeing you face-to-face.

But whatever were gains to me I now consider loss for the sake of Christ. What is more, I consider everything a loss because of the surpassing worth of knowing Christ Jesus my Lord, for whose sake I have lost all things. I consider them garbage, that I may gain Christ and be found in him, not having a righteousness of my own that comes from the law, but that which is through faith in Christ—the righteousness that comes from God on the basis of faith. I want to know Christ—yes, to know the power of his resurrection and participation in his sufferings, becoming like him in his death, and so, somehow, attaining to the resurrection from the dead.

PHILIPPIANS 3:7-11 (NIV)

Lord,

I desire to suffer well in this season and grasp that there is a purpose in every struggle that comes my way. Even if I have to give up everything the world offers, I desire to know you more.

May I:
 believe better
  endure anything
   find strength in the hope that is to come

You:
 Suffered well, first
  Desire that I know you completely
   Have made resurrection power available to me

 As a result, I consider everything else a poor
substitute for life with you now and
the promise of heaven to come.
By faith I am knowing and
experiencing your power daily.
You are the true prize.

threadbare prayer:

LORD, nothing compares with knowing you.

Fear not, for I am with you;
be not dismayed, for I am your God;
I will strengthen you, I will help you,
I will uphold you with my righteous right hand.

ISAIAH 41:10

Lord,

My fear sometimes blinds me to the fact that you are not far off but very close. Fear wants me to feel alone so I will not reach out and take you by the hand.

I am:
    chosen
        gathered from the ends of the earth
            as close to you as I can get

You:
    Give me courage
        Help me
            Hold me steady

I can't fill my heart with thoughts of you and continue to be afraid. The promise of your nearness is an arrow straight to the heart of every faith-crippling fear. Truly God will strengthen me. He alone will help me, and fear will have no part of my heart.

threadbare prayer:

LORD, when I choose to focus on your nearness, fear has to flee.

So that you may live a life worthy of the Lord and please him in every way: bearing fruit in every good work, growing in the knowledge of God, being strengthened with all power according to his glorious might so that you may have great endurance and patience, and giving joyful thanks to the Father, who has qualified you to share in the inheritance of his holy people in the kingdom of light.

COLOSSIANS 1:10-12 (NIV)

Lord,

I know that when I encounter trials other people might be watching to see how I handle them as your daughter. I want to walk with you in a way that brings other people into the kingdom of light.

I will:

    pray without stopping

        seek to live in a way that honors you

            give thanks no matter what

You:

    Give me glory-strength

        Render me fit

            Offer me fellowship in the light

A worthy walk looks like joy, patience, and endurance that brings honor to your name even on the hardest days. Even in times of significant distress, I pray I will draw on your glory-strength and my outward life will be an overflow with what you are doing on the inside.

threadbare prayer:

LORD, I want my life to always be a credit to you.

*so that your faith might not rest
in the wisdom of men but in the power of God.*

1 Corinthians 2:5

Lord,

It is amazing to me that my threadbare moments can actually be used by you. No one is going to look at me and think, "Wow, she has it all together." Instead, they will see you working and say, "Her God is strong." And that is exactly how it should be.

I am not:
impressive
bold
eloquent

You are:
Wise beyond words
Full of miraculous power
Always working

If you can use me as I am. I pray that you will. But mostly, I don't ever want to get in the way of what you are doing.

I don't want to be a distraction or discouragement to your purpose and plan. The good news is an empty vessel needs to be filled with something, and I am seeking to be filled with you so that is all others will notice.

threadbare prayer:

LORD, let others see you, not me.

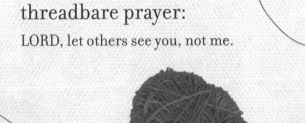

Count it all joy, my brothers, when you meet
trials of various kinds, for you know that
the testing of your faith produces steadfastness.
And let steadfastness have its full effect, that you
may be perfect and complete, lacking in nothing.

JAMES 1:2-4

Lord,

I confess to you that my first response is not to embrace trials as joy-filled gifts. I usually complain and resist them thinking there must be some mistake. I'm grateful you are patient with me.

I:
    naturally resist trials
        want to see hard seasons as faith training
            need to be steadfast every day

You:
    Allow trials to test my faith
        Provide me opportunities to grow in patience
            Desire my character to lack nothing

I should know by now that if you send the trial to train my faith, my best course of action is to be grateful. Every time my faith is tested it is an opportunity to linger in your presence. You love me enough to work in me in good times and bad and it will be worth it.

threadbare prayer:

LORD, I want to see trials as gifts that draw me closer to you.

*"And his name will be the hope of
all the world."*

MATTHEW 12:21, NLT

Lord,

It was your love for us that moved you to do the unthinkable. To wrap your all-knowing, all-loving, all-gracious God-sized heart in human flesh. You became like us, to love us in our own language.

I am:
> humbled by your coming
>> looking for fresh hope
>>> overwhelmed by grace

You:
> Came
>> Are the hope of all the world
>>> Will come again

I ask that you once again ignite hope in my heart. Burn bright in my life so that hope will light the way for others who are broken in a world that is heavy and holding its breath.

threadbare prayer:

LORD, hope of all the world, burn bright in me.

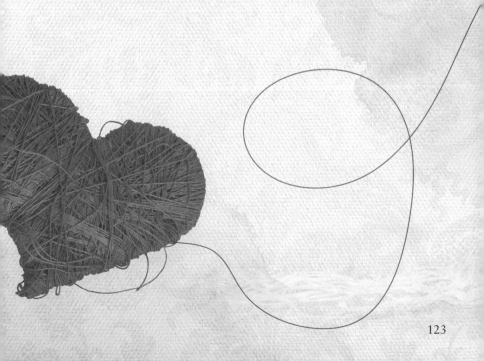

"Yours, O Lord, is the greatness, the power, the glory, the victory, and the majesty. Everything in the heavens and on earth is yours, O Lord, and this is your kingdom. We adore you as the one who is over all things."

1 Chronicles 29:11 (NLT)

Lord,

Worship reminds me that you are God and I am not. This is your kingdom and you deserve all the honor and glory.

I am:
   small
      reaching for you
         surrendered in worship

You are:
   Great
      Glorious
         Ruling over all things

   Adoration of you changes me in the best possible way. Suddenly, I am no longer wandering, restless, and focused on myself. I look around and see that any kingdom I have tried to build on my own is worthless compared to knowing and serving you. You alone are worthy.

threadbare prayer:

LORD, adoring you changes me.

But this I call to mind,
and therefore I have hope:
The steadfast love of the LORD never ceases;
his mercies never come to an end;
they are new every morning;
great is your faithfulness.
"The LORD is my portion," says my soul,
"therefore I will hope in him."

<small>LAMENTATIONS 3:21-24</small>

Lord,

One sure way to stir up my hope is to remember when I've had troubles before, your kindness has never failed.

I am:
remembering what you have done
hanging onto hope
trusting you with what will happen

You:
Have never-ending loving-kindness for me
Do not fail
Are enough for me

You don't have to wake me up and show me your mercies each morning, but you do anyway. In you I have exactly what my soul needs and this is where I will stake my hope claim. Even if I lose what the world thinks is important, I will never lose what I have in you. It is good for me to remember your faithfulness over and over again.

threadbare prayer:

LORD, I will remember you have always been faithful.

*"…And do not be grieved,
for the joy of the LORD is your strength."*

NEHEMIAH 8:10

Lord,

Weeping may last for a season, but joy comes when I take your Word to heart and let it comfort me right where I am. You are a patient friend when all I have are tears for what might have been.

I am:
struggling to let go of the past
sorry
wrestling a spirit of heaviness

You say:
Weep no more
This is the time for joy
My strength is yours

You are not ashamed of me but pull me close and say, "Dry your tears and let this mourning become fertile ground for my abundant joy over you. Let that make you strong." Slowly, as I let your joy wash over me and take root, quiet yet solid strength rises up and takes me with it out of the depths and into the light of a new day.

threadbare prayer:

LORD, your joy makes me strong.

Praise be to the LORD,
for he has heard my cry for mercy.
The LORD is my strength and my shield;
my heart trusts in him, and he helps me.
My heart leaps for joy,
and with my song I praise him.

PSALM 28:6-7 (NIV)

Lord,

When I cry for help, you come running with everything I need. If I need comfort, you are there. If I need protection, you are there. If I need help. you are my portion. There is nothing I need that you can't provide.

I:
    call to you
        feel safe
            praise you

You:
    Hear me
        Are my source of strength
            Cover me

When you come, I'm not crying for mercy, I'm singing your praise. I am able to be careless in your care with joy that is evident. Only you can enter a seemingly hopeless situation and transform my heart from tears to triumph.

threadbare prayer:

LORD, I am careless in your care, and that is worth singing about.

Now to him who is able to keep you from stumbling and to present you blameless before the presence of his glory with great joy, to the only God, our Savior, through Jesus Christ our Lord, be glory, majesty, dominion, and authority, before all time and now and forever. Amen.

JUDE 24-25

Lord,

When I am discouraged, defeated, and convinced there is no way out, I need to saturate my mind with your character. Looking to you, my situation will not seem so hopeless because you certainly are not.

I:

am kept from falling away

am brought blameless into your glorious presence

give you all the glory

You:

Alone are God

Saved us through Christ

Contain all majesty, power, and authority

You are able to keep me from stumbling and present me before your majestic throne without stain or blemish. You say through Christ I'm blameless in your presence and for that and everything else, I will give you all the glory.

threadbare prayer:

LORD, I will give you all the glory.

Let us then with confidence draw near
to the throne of grace, that we may receive mercy
and find grace to help in time of need.

HEBREWS 4:16

Lord,

Your invitation is clear. The door is always open to your holy place. When I come, I am able to get the very things I need most—your endless mercy and your sustaining grace.

I:
> do not need to be afraid
>> can walk into your presence
>>> find favor

You:
> sit on a throne of grace
>> invite me in
>>> pour out mercy for my failures

The reason I can step boldly into your presence is that you made a way once and for all through your death on the cross. You removed the barrier of sin and separation as far as the east is from the west. I will not forget that opening that door cost you everything. So, I come.

threadbare prayer:

LORD, I come to you because I can.

The LORD is a stronghold for the oppressed,
a stronghold in times of trouble.
And those who know your name put their trust in you,
for you, O LORD, have not forsaken those who seek you.

PSALM 9:9-10

Lord,

    When my heart is crushed by burdens of this world, I take great comfort in knowing I can come to you any time. You provide a high place in the stronghold of your arms for me to be lifted out of the destruction I see all around me.

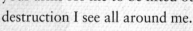

I am:
   miserable
      afflicted
         seeking you

You:
   Are comforting
     Are healing
        Do not abandon me

Loving and knowing your name grows my trust in you because you never abandon a heart that searches for you. The more I know you, the more I seek you, and find you faithful. This is your precious promise to me.

threadbare prayer:

LORD, I keep seeking and you keep sheltering.

"Be still, and know that I am God.
I will be exalted among the nations,
I will be exalted in the earth!"

PSALM 46:10

Lord,

Being still is not my typical reaction when there is a battle raging all around me. Quite the opposite is true because it sets my anxious heart on edge. But I can choose to be calm. knowing that you are in control and I don't have to be.

I am:
at war
troubled
shaken

You Are:
Mighty to save
Ready to help
Present with me

God, you know how and when to move in my life. I marvel at the fact that you are never stressed or worried about what will happen. Considering this, I can take my hands off this situation, stop stressing, and let you be the True God— knowing I'm not and I don't have to be.

threadbare prayer:
LORD, I will let go, and let you be God.

Jesus answered him, "What I am doing you do not understand now, but afterward you will understand."

Lord,

From where I sit, I can't comprehend what you are doing in my life. Many times, you don't explain it but ask me to trust that you know best. I want to shout, *"This can't be the way. Are you sure this is your plan?"* It seems to me there has to be a better path than this.

I am:
    limited in perspective
        confused by circumstances
            doubtful all will be well

You:
    Have a plan
        Will choose what is best
            Ask me to simply trust you

Tenderly, through your Word, you whisper to my doubts. "I know you don't understand what I'm doing today, but when you look back on even this, you will see that I had your best interest at heart and my plan was the way to go." Today it is enough to know that later my "why" will turn into "of course that is what you were doing."

threadbare prayer:

LORD, I don't understand now, but someday I will.

*For God gave us a spirit not of fear
but of power and love and self-control.*

2 TIMOTHY 1:7

Lord,

More days than not, around 4 a.m., I wake up with the feeling that fear is like a person, actually sitting on my chest hurling "what ifs" at my heart with precision. I don't want fear to be my battle. But lately, it has been.

I:
    feel exposed
        sense chaos rising
            see the worst-case scenario

You:
    Fill me with your Spirit
        Give me courage
            Create calm

When fear comes calling, you want me to go to your Word. When I read it, you stir up the flame of faith filling me with love, courage, and God-sized power. I realize now that I do have a choice. Fear is a bully I won't yield to anymore.

threadbare prayer:

LORD, you fill me with love, power, and calmness of heart.

Jesus Christ is the same yesterday and today and forever.

HEBREWS 13:8

Lord,

Change seems to be inevitable. Except when it applies to you. There is great comfort in knowing the God I find in Genesis, Psalms, and Romans is my God too. I don't have to wonder how you will act in my life because I can watch how you interacted with countless people in the Bible.

I am:
comforted
anchored
settled

You Are:
Savior
Anointed
Changeless

You will always be with me and provide everything I will ever need. In you, there are no shifting sands. Instead I have an anchor that does not fail, firmly planted in the unchangeableness of your rock-solid character. The world can change in a heartbeat, but you will always be the same loving and faithful God.

threadbare prayer:

LORD, you do not change.

See what kind of love the Father has given to us,
that we should be called children of God;
and so we are. The reason why the world
does not know us is that it did not know him.

1 JOHN 3:1

Lord,

The extravagant love you have for me
keeps me mindful of what it means to be
your beloved daughter. You have never
hidden your love for your children.
You delight in putting it on
display for the world
to see.

I am:
>>a beloved child
>>>>named by the Father
>>>>>>stranger to the world

You are:
>>The One who reconciles
>>>>Pouring out abundant love
>>>>>>Claiming me as your own

Incredible as it is, you have chosen me and lavished me with a sacrificial and everlasting love that changes me from the inside out. I am named and deeply known by you. This is all this beloved daughter needs today.

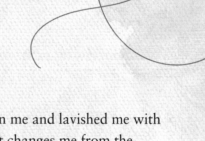

threadbare prayer:

LORD, your love is extravagant.

As far as the east is from the west,
so far does he remove our transgressions from us.

PSALM 103:12

Lord,

I can buy into the fact that I am loved. I can put a couple of great days back to back and think I'm not so bad. But then, it happens. I have one of those no-good, awful, horrible bad days, and I blow it. What happens when my fear of failure turns into failure?

I:
> yelled at my family
>> bent the truth
>>> judged others

You:
> Tenderly call out to me
>> Have already forgiven me
>>> Separated me from my sins

While I am swimming in the sea of my own guilt and shame, you quietly say, *"I want you to know, I think of you as already forgiven."* And then, you smile, and stretch out your arms and say, *"I've removed it as far as the east is from the west. It is gone. I carried away. So there would not be anything between us ever again."* I could try to measure the extent of your forgiveness, but east to west gets me every time.

threadbare prayer:

LORD, you remove my sin so there is nothing between us.

I didn't have long passages of Scripture. I had a single verse. It was enough.

What Shatters
and What Holds

My youngest daughter dropped my iPad just before I hurried out the door to go to church. With huge tears streaming down her face she pulled it from behind her back and sobbed, *"I'm sorry, Mommy, I broke it."* For some reason I didn't lose my mind over the shattering. I hugged her with a sigh of surrender, *"Don't worry about it. These things happen. We'll talk to Daddy about it later when he gets home. Maybe he knows how to fix it."*

But, later never came. A few hours later, her daddy was in the ICU fighting for his life and fixing the broken electronic was forgotten. Obviously.

Broken. Shattered. Fix it.

I was in a worship service at church when my husband's heart stopped during a business meeting

across town. On a random night in February 2017, Mike was rushed to the hospital while I was worshipping God and singing:

Holy, holy are you Lord God almighty.
*Worthy is the Lamb.**

When I finally got to him and understood the gravity of the situation, my heart stopped, too, but in an entirely different way. I went numb—and began to shake. Breathing became my focus. And my world became very small.

Sit down.
Drink a cup of water.
Call the girls.
Answer questions.
Repeat.

I didn't run from suffering because I couldn't move. But I wasn't exactly embracing it either. Oh, I

*"Agnus Dei," by Michael W. Smith,
Copyright © 1990 Sony/ATV Tunes, LLC.
All rights admin. by Sony/ATV Music Publishing.

knew suffering. We had been around the block more than a few times. I wasn't walking bravely on oceans this time. I was once again weeping in the desert.

Familiar ground.

This desert, I've learned the hard way, is where the redeemed learn to walk (Isaiah 35:9). I have spent more days here than I care to count. I haven't chosen to walk here. But over and over again it has become the path beneath my feet. This time I wasn't sure I was actually going to walk at all, let alone find the gateway of hope. How can you walk when you can't move or feel your own feet beneath you? **And somehow in the cold, hard chair of the ICU waiting room I got it.** Stripped bare and waiting. *Again.* My undoing, now severe and complete, I reached out to Jesus with the first threadbare prayer I remember praying.

The LORD is my shepherd;
I have everything I need.
    Psalm 23:1 (GNT)

The only Bible I had within reach was a Children's version. I flipped the colorful pages to this passage and could not read past the first verse of this familiar funeral Psalm. I didn't have

any eloquent words for Jesus. I didn't have long passages of Scripture. I had a single verse. It was enough.

I preached that verse over and over to my soul that first night, the next morning, and then again all day Saturday when they told me it was bad. *Very bad.* **I breathed it in and breathed it out in the midst of the valley of the shadow of death for an entire month.** It wasn't that I didn't believe it in my head. I did. But, my heart needed to be sure that when I broke apart completely it would hold.

I broke. But my Shepherd did not.

He held in every moment of fear, numbness, and through every step of our healing journey. He kept pressing his promise to my heart.

I am your shepherd. You have everything you need.

It seems simple doesn't it? Jesus didn't complicate his provision with my need. This truth has become a constant cadence in my life. The sound of me needing him and him being absolutely enough has become my heartbeat.

The Lord is my shepherd; I have everything I need.
He is all I need today when I'm not sure how I'm going

to help my husband heal, take care of my girls, and figure out how to pay the bills. He will be all I need the next time something breaks and I have no control of the outcome. We both know it will, too. Because we live in a world that breaks, shatters, and cries out, "Fix it." Every day. *Lord Jesus, our shepherd, be near.*

His Word is our promise. He is our truth. He does not break. He breaks through.

He holds.

Always.

And the effect of righteousness will be peace,
and the result of righteousness, quietness and trust forever.
My people will abide in a peaceful habitation,
in secure dwellings, and in quiet resting places.

ISAIAH 32:17-18

Lord,

Your Word is packed with truth that I can take to heart
as I seek to do your will. I will consider your promise that
better days are coming, especially when I
can't see my way through a trial that
seems relentless.

I:

    seek to do what is right

        remember your promises

            trust you

You:

    Rule as a righteous king

        Offer me inward peace

            Provide a safe dwelling place

Though it would be easy to focus on the turmoil threatening to overtake me, I can choose to be at ease in my heart with a supernatural peace of mind that only comes from you. I can also look around and take comfort in the promise that I am safe and secure because you are my king forever. You hold my future in your hands. You make my home a secure place. I don't have to be afraid of anything.

threadbare prayer:

Lord, I trust better days are coming.

Strengthen the weak hands,
and make firm the feeble knees.
Say to those who have an anxious heart,
"Be strong; fear not!
Behold, your God
will come with vengeance,
with the recompense of God.
He will come and save you."

ISAIAH 35:3-4

Lord,

In this wilderness place I've
dropped the ball too many times
to count because I can't hold on.
My faith has stretched thin and I feel
like I might literally collapse to the floor. I
don't think I can stand on my own two feet, let alone
walk the path you have set before me. It is precisely here
that you declare that I will see your glory on display.

I am:
   faint-hearted
      tired
         anxious

You say:
   Be restored
      Have courage
         I am coming to save you and set things right

    This is the heart of the Gospel—you have come. You are coming. You won't stop coming to strengthen my anxious heart. And like a drumbeat through the ages you keep saying, "Be strong, fear not! I am mighty to save. You can count on me." Weak hands and feeble knees need not be afraid with you here and on the way.

threadbare prayer:

LORD, I will not fear because I can count on you.

For freedom Christ has set us free; stand firm therefore,
and do not submit again to a yoke of slavery.

GALATIANS 5:1

Lord,

    I don't want to go back to the sin of self-sufficiency that easily entangles my heart. You completely and fully liberated me from that sin when you died on the cross for me. You want me to know how freedom feels and looks and that it can transform my day-to-day life.

I am free:
    from worry
        from being a slave to "should"
            to live for you

You:
    Satisfied the law completely
        Set me free
            Died to make it true

This tired-of-doing and people-pleasing girl needs constant reminders to run back to your Word and your freedom ways. You set me free so that I will continue to live in freedom, not run back to the bondage of my sin. Today, I will take hold of your hand, breathe deep, and stand in the freedom you have already given me.

threadbare prayer:

Lord, I will stay free because you made me free.

For
"All flesh is like grass
and all its glory like the flower of grass.
The grass withers,
and the flower falls,
but the word of the Lord remains forever."
And this word is the good news that was preached to you.

1 Peter 1:24-25

Lord,

It is easy to get discouraged by how fragile life can be. I
wish I could fix all the broken pieces I
see all around me. I need to make a
habit of coming again and again
to the solidness of your Word so I
can encourage my heart with your
unchanging truth.

I see:
    uncertainty
        life fading
            a withering world

Your Word:
    Is perpetual
        Does not fail
            Provides a sense of security

The same Word I hold in my hands was declared by your prophets of old, completely fulfilled in Jesus, and proclaimed by the apostles. Your Word does not change. When life withers and fades as I know it will, I need to keep my eyes fixed on your always forever enduring Word.

threadbare prayer:

LORD, when my world withers, your Word remains.

*"Though the mountains be shaken
and the hills be removed,
yet my unfailing love for you will not be shaken
nor my covenant of peace be removed,"
says the LORD, who has compassion on you.*

ISAIAH 54:10 (NIV)

Lord,

The love you have for me is altogether different from any
I have ever experienced in my life. You do not base your
love on what I do or who I am.
Your love does not fade. It is
patient and always on display.
You speak about it over and
over again in your Word to
encourage my heart.

I wonder:
> why you love me
>> if it will ever run out
>>> what I can do to earn it

You say:
> I will not desert you.
>> My love will not be shaken
>>> My love does not depend on your behavior

You picked the most awesome of your creations to illustrate how you love me. The mountains don't seem to be going anywhere. But if they crumble into the heart of the sea, even then, your love will never shake loose of me. You won't walk away because your love doesn't ever give up.

threadbare prayer:

LORD, your love does not walk away from me.

And after you have suffered a little while, the God of all grace, who has called you to his eternal glory in Christ, will himself restore, confirm, strengthen, and establish you.

1 PETER 5:10

Lord,

Suffering doesn't feel brief when you are in it. It seems achingly slow. Yet, I can be sure that if you have allowed this trial, there is a purpose in it and your promise is to see me through. Since you have me here, I trust that this season will only last as long as you deem necessary.

I am:
    suffering
        counting the minutes of "a little while"
            surrendering to your will

You promise to:
    Restore
        Confirm
            Steady me

Your merciful kindness leads me step-by-step towards the time when all will be made well. You are making all things new and that includes me. This too will pass and what remains will be your grace and glory.

threadbare prayer:

LORD, all will be well in a little while.

saying,
"I called out to the LORD, out of my distress,
and he answered me;
out of the belly of Sheol I cried,
and you heard my voice."

JONAH 2:2

Lord,

When I am at my lowest possible moment, you do not turn from me like most people do. You are closer than I can imagine and waiting for me to call out to you.

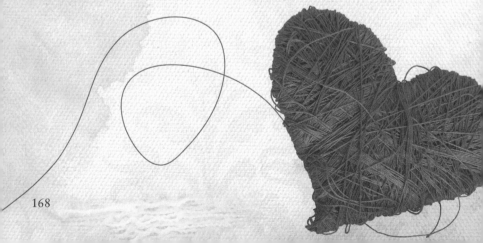

I am:
    deeply troubled
        as low as I can get
            crying out to you

You:
    Are near
        Listen for my cry
            Respond when I call

    It doesn't matter if I'm in the belly of a whale or on my bathroom floor crying out to you. These low places are not lonely places because you are here too. I need to remember that I am never too far gone to cry out to you and you will hear me.

threadbare prayer:

LORD, I am never beyond your reach.

"I have said these things to you, that in me you may have peace. In the world you will have tribulation. But take heart; I have overcome the world."

JOHN 16:33

Lord,

I can trust you to always tell me the truth. You don't sugarcoat the hardships in life or try to keep me from wrestling with them. You honestly say in your Word—in this world you will have times of trouble. I should never be surprised when troubles inevitably come.

I:
    see trouble all around me
        have had times of trials
            expect difficulties in the future

You:
    Tell me the truth to prepare me
        Want me to be at peace
            Have overcome the world

I can choose to be wholly at peace and unshakable when I face seemingly impossible situations. The reason for such confidence is that you experienced troubles of every kind and at the same time you have already defeated the enemy of this godless world. I can abide in that victory knowing that in you I overcome it all too.

threadbare prayer:

LORD, I will not lose heart because you have overcome the world.

Trust in the LORD with all your heart,
and do not lean on your own understanding.
In all your ways acknowledge him,
and he will make straight your paths.

PROVERBS 3:5-6

Lord,

My default tendency is
to try to fix what is not
working. I like to feel like I
am in control of my life, my
choices, and my future. But
I know, deep within my heart,
that my need to be calling the
shots is really rooted in my lack of
trust in you.

I:
    realize I control nothing
        understand I need to completely trust you
            submit my way entirely to you

You:
    Are worthy of my trust
        Direct my steps
            Keep me on the right path

When I stop gritting my teeth and let go of my sense of control, I am able to lean into your trustworthiness. It is here I experience a peace and protection as I walk along the way you have established for me. I don't have to worry what will happen because I know you have gone ahead of me clearing and straightening my path.

threadbare prayer:

LORD, I will lean into your trustworthiness, not my need for control.

Though the fig tree should not blossom,
nor fruit be on the vines,
the produce of the olive fail
and the fields yield no food,
the flock be cut off from the fold
and there be no herd in the stalls,
yet I will rejoice in the LORD;
I will take joy in the God of my salvation.

HABAKKUK 3:17-18

Lord,

If I simply judge my future by what I can see, everyday life can look pretty discouraging. I know, however, from experience that there is more happening than meets my eyes.

I see:
    broken dreams
        failure
            emptiness

You:
    Are the self-existing One
        Are the True God
            Deliver me

When things look the worst, I need to shift my focus and remember I can't lose what really matters. As I believe better, my feelings of discouragement grow smaller and smaller. In the process, my emptiness hollows out a place that is filled with great joy and become a blessing to others.

threadbare prayer:

LORD, even if I lose everything, I will never lose what I have in you.

*"In this you rejoice, though now for a little while,
if necessary, you have been grieved by various trials,
so that the tested genuineness of your faith—more precious
than gold that perishes though it is tested by fire—
may be found to result in praise and glory
and honor at the revelation of Jesus Christ."*

1 PETER 1:6-7

Lord,

I can be sure that this season of suffering is not an
accident. You have not misplaced me or left me to take
care of this all on my own. You are here working out
my faith in the midst of my hardest days.

I can:
> find joy in the junk
>> let you test my faith
>>> look forward to what will be revealed

You:
> Use trials to refine me
>> Limit my trials to a season
>>> Will display my faith to glorify your name

You purpose in allowing this trial is to refine my faith so that the junk falls away and what remains has genuine value to you. When others see me come through this season, my hope is that I am changed and you are glorified. This is the real reason to rejoice.

threadbare prayer:

LORD, I can find true joy in the junk.

*"The secret things belong to the L*ORD *our God,*
but the things that are revealed belong to us and to our
children forever, that we may do all the words of this law."

DEUTERONOMY 29:29

Lord,

I often find myself asking you "Why?" when I know
full well you rarely give me the answer to that question.
A better question for me to ask is, "What do you want me
to learn?" That is a question you delight in answering and
keeps me focused on what really matters.

I:
    ask why
        can know some things
            will never know other things

You:
    Take care of secret things
        Reveal truth
            Keep your promises to generations forever

The beautiful mystery I need to remember is that what you have hidden I don't really need to know. At the same time, I can be confident knowing that what you have revealed saves me and sustains me every single day. That is enough for me.

threadbare prayer:

LORD, what you have hidden I don't need to know.

Then he opened their minds to understand the Scriptures.

LUKE 24:45

Lord,

Your Word lights up the path I am to take. By it, you encourage my heart and convict me of sin that weighs me down and wears me out. Your Word is how I make sense of the world and find the hope I need to live in it.

I:

    can study your Word

        must make my time in the Word a priority

            seek understanding

Your Spirit:

    Opens my mind

        Understands what I am thinking

            Interprets the text for me

There is no book like yours. It stands out uniquely because when I read it, you meet me and breathe life into my soul. Only you can unveil my eyes to understand your truth at the deepest level. Show me today how to read it and apply it to my life. I want to be changed today in the best way possible.

threadbare prayer:

LORD, unveil my eyes so I understand your Word.

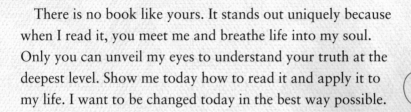

On the last day of the feast, the great day, Jesus stood up and cried out, "If anyone thirsts, let him come to me and drink. Whoever believes in me, as the Scripture has said, 'Out of his heart will flow rivers of living water.'"

Lord,

I long for a quiet place in my life. A place to sit and just be given refreshment for soul and body too. I feel by the end of my very long days, like a dried up well. Yet each morning, when the horrible sound of the alarm pierces my sleep-deprived body, I am tempted to ignore it time and time again.

I come:
    thirsty
        weary
            longing for quiet

You:
    Wait for me
        Invite me to come to you
            Offer me living water

I realize that if I am going to make it today with any life left in me, I have to meet with you first. When I do this, I receive a beautiful exchange. I give you my weary soul, and you pour fresh life-giving water from your ever-flowing spring of joy into me that then overflows to others.

threadbare prayer:

Lord when I come thirsty, you always pour out
life-giving water.

But when he saw the wind, he was afraid,
and beginning to sink he cried out, "Lord, save me." Jesus
immediately reached out his hand and took hold of him,
saying to him, "O you of little faith, why did you doubt?"
And when they got into the boat, the wind ceased.

MATTHEW 14:30-32

Lord,

I want to have courageous faith. I want to be one who boldly takes your Word and is willing to bravely step out of the boat onto the water. I don't want to be affected by the sight of the wind and waves, but often my shallow faith leaves me fearful and sinking fast.

I:
want faith to step out
see the storm around me
start to sink

You:
Hear me cry out
Calm the storm
Take hold of me

All this time I've been scrambling to get back in the boat and what you have been offering me is yourself. In the millisecond I am going under and cry out to you, you don't hesitate to take hold of me. Truly, the comfort of the boat holds nothing compared to the refuge of your embrace.

threadbare prayer:

LORD, when I am going under, you take hold of me.

For God alone, O my soul, wait in silence,
for my hope is from him.
He only is my rock and my salvation,
my fortress; I shall not be shaken.
On God rests my salvation and my glory;
my mighty rock, my refuge is God.
Trust in him at all times, O people;
pour out your heart before him;
God is a refuge for us. Selah

PSALM 62:5-8

Lord,

My hope comes only from
you. But today, I'm struggling
to feel hopeful at all. If I'm
honest I don't really want to pray
right now. I have learned when I don't
want to pray, I need to pray more than ever.

I am:
    struggling to feel hope
        pouring out my heart
            waiting in silence

You are:
    My help
        My true source of strength
            My safe place

Because of who you are, I am praying and waiting for you alone. I am here, laying out my heart before you, sharing my doubts, shouting my ache, and leaning into the shelter of your arms. I know that when I am shaken and discouraged, the safest place to be found is in your presence.

threadbare prayer:

LORD, I trust you to be a safe place for my heart.

"O Lord, let your ear be attentive to the prayer of your servant, and to the prayer of your servants who delight to fear your name, and give success to your servant today, and grant him mercy in the sight of this man."

NEHEMIAH 1:11

Lord,

I willingly worship you today as the One who is sovereign over every event in my life. You are also a wise Father who provides and protects those who love and honor you. Because you are master over everything, I know you are the one I need to surrender to today.

I am:
    your servant
        humbled in your presence
            seeking your favor

You are:
    LORD
        Master
            Compassionate

Please listen eagerly to my request for success today as I go where you want me to go and do what you want me to do. I do not go in my own name—I walk in yours with all that it carries. If you are willing, give me favor today in the eyes of those you have put in authority over me. They answer to you ultimately, LORD, master over everything.

threadbare prayer:

LORD, if you are willing, give me favor today for your name's sake.

"But he knows the way that I take;
when he has tried me, I shall come out as gold.
My foot has held fast to his steps;
I have kept his way and have not turned aside.
I have not departed from the commandment of his lips;
I have treasured the words of his mouth more than my
portion of food."

Job 23:10-12

Lord,

You know where I am going, even if I can't see where
I will end up. What I do know for sure is that even if the
path you mark out leads me through times of
testing, you are not being cruel. I have your
Word as a promise and protector of
my heart.

I:
> have chosen your way
>> closely followed your leading
>>> cherished your Word

You:
> Know the way I take
>> Mark the steps for me
>>> Do not lose sight of me

In your Word, you have set boundaries to testing places and promise they will come to an end. On the other side of it, I have the benefit of knowing I will be better for it. Your Word is a treasure, and I will not swerve sideways from what it says no matter how hard things get.

threadbare prayer:

LORD, treasuring your Word keeps me on the right path.

The LORD will fulfill his purpose for me;
your steadfast love, O LORD, endures forever.
Do not forsake the work of your hands.

PSALM 138:8

Lord,

You are a deeply personal God who could sit on his throne and keep your distance. But, instead you are continually pursuing and perfecting that which concerns your children—including me. Oh, how grateful I am that you are who you are!

I am:
> humbled by your notice of me
>> strengthened by your steadfast love
>>> joining you in the work you are doing

You:
> Are great and glorious
>> Regard the lowly
>>> Finish what you start

    With compassionate loving-kindness you begin a work in my life and bring it to a beautiful completion. You don't leave me undone or defenseless. Your steadfastness draws my heart to cooperate with the work you are doing and trust the process.

threadbare prayer:

LORD, I will trust the process because you finish what you start.

Now to him who is able to do far more abundantly than all that we ask or think, according to the power at work within us, to him be glory in the church and in Christ Jesus throughout all generations, forever and ever. Amen.

EPHESIANS 3:20-21

Lord,

You are able to do a work in my life that is far beyond my wildest dreams and then you are able to do still more. In fact, I can't even ask for what you are able to do, because my mind can't conceive of it.

I am:
    rooted and grounded in your love
        strengthened by grace
            filled with the fullness of God

You:
    Are able to do anything
        Work deeply and gently within me
            Deserve all the glory

Much of the time, I fail to see that the greater work you are doing isn't in my circumstances, but in what you are doing within me. Gently you work wonders in the small hidden places of my heart, and then you choose to graciously work through me. This is a glorious gift that is more than I could ask for or imagine.

threadbare prayer:

LORD, you are abundantly able and choose to
work within me.

*Brothers and sisters, I do not consider myself
yet to have taken hold of it. But one thing I do:
Forgetting what is behind and straining toward what is
ahead, I press on toward the goal to win the prize for
which God has called me heavenward in Christ Jesus.*

PHILIPPIANS 3:13-14 (NIV)

Lord,

I can't go back and ask for a do-over, although part of me wishes I could. At the same time, I don't have all the answers even now. I'm here in this middle ground with a decision to make. I can look at the past and hold on to regrets, or I can face forward and run with abandon towards the finish line.

I:

    have not arrived

        will leave my old life behind

            reach for the goal of knowing Jesus

You:

    Have forgiven every mistake I've made

        Are calling me forward

            Have gone before me

    I won't be stopped by past sins, discouragements, or others who want to hold me back. I will press on eagerly running towards you with arms open wide until I reach my goal all for your glory.

threadbare prayer:

LORD, I will press onward and not turn back.

For the word of God is living and active, sharper than any two-edged sword, piercing to the division of soul and of spirit, of joints and of marrow, and discerning the thoughts and intentions of the heart. And no creature is hidden from his sight, but all are naked and exposed to the eyes of him to whom we must give account.

HEBREWS 4:12-13

Lord,

Your Word is not like any other book. It has a life-giving effect on me when I read it because you are present and with me, helping me to understand what it says. Your Word is what my threadbare heart needs most.

I:
open your Word
meet with you
am wholly restored

Your Word:
Is living
Is powerful
Exposes my heart

I am both drawn to your Word with hope and approach it
with a holy fear. I can't hide from you when I read it because
it cuts to the heart of the matter, revealing my thoughts, fears,
and secret sins. But you first wound that you might heal me.
Thankfully, your all-powerful Word does both.

threadbare prayer:

LORD, may your Word do something in me, to me,
and through me.

God did this so that, by two unchangeable things in which it is impossible for God to lie, we who have fled to take hold of the hope set before us may be greatly encouraged. We have this hope as an anchor for the soul, firm and secure. It enters the inner sanctuary behind the curtain, where our forerunner, Jesus, has entered on our behalf.

HEBREWS 6:18-20 (NIV)

Lord,

Your changelessness is a stark contrast to the world around me. There is always something new and different to take in or try to understand. But in the swirl of ever-changing uncertainty, you remain the same and steady me.

I am:
    seeing the winds of culture
        rocked by waves of uncertainty
            looking for something to hold on to

You:
    Do not change
        Do not lie
            Are secure

You do not lie or bend the truth. Because you willingly put your life on the line to prove it, I can run to you and hold on to your promises. You are a strong anchor that will hold steady and true when society spins out of control.

threadbare prayer:

LORD, you are a steadfast anchor for my soul.

> *"Blessed rather are those who*
> *hear the word of God and keep it!"*
>
> Luke 11:28

Lord,

I think you gave us your Word so that we would always have the truth of who you are and what you did right in front of us. If I have a question, I can search it out. If I am discouraged, I can read about your great love. And if I need my hope ignited, I simply have to open your book.

I:

    have access to your Word

        consider what you say

            will make it my way of life

You:

    Are the Word made flesh

        Dwelled among us

            Blessed us by writing it down

The enemy doesn't want me to hear your Word, let alone for it to take root in my heart or be fruitful. He wants to steal it away. But I will guard it with my whole life knowing that when I do, you will richly bless my life.

threadbare prayer:

LORD, I will guard your Word with my life.

*Blessed be the God and Father of our Lord Jesus Christ!
According to his great mercy, he has caused us
to be born again to a living hope through the
resurrection of Jesus Christ from the dead, to an
inheritance that is imperishable, undefiled,
and unfading, kept in heaven for you.*

1 PETER 1:3-4

Lord,

The living hope you give me is
not like the world's whimsical
version. My hope is infused with
the power that raised you from the
grave to declare victory over my
sin-weary heart.

I:

> was saved by a living hope
>> am being strengthened right now by hope
>>> have a certain future filled with hope

You:

> Have boundless mercy
>> Are the author of ever-living hope
>>> You keep hope securely in heaven for me

With you, I can never be hopeless. When I am tempted to give up, living hope energizes my soul because of what you have done, what you are doing, and what is waiting for me in heaven that will never be destroyed or fade away.

threadbare prayer:

LORD, living hope means I am never hopeless.

But he said to me, "My grace is sufficient for you, for my power is made perfect in weakness." Therefore I will boast all the more gladly of my weaknesses, so that the power of Christ may rest upon me. For the sake of Christ, then, I am content with weaknesses, insults, hardships, persecutions, and calamities. For when I am weak, then I am strong.

2 CORINTHIANS 12:9-10

Lord,

I am afraid of my own weakness, but you are not. Your grace promise is that I will have exactly what I need when I need it. Your sufficiency flows from your endless source of strength.

I am:
  weak
    breathing out clumsy prayers asking for help
      afraid of what others might think of me

Your Grace:
  Is sufficient
    Is always available
      Is powerfully perfect in my weakness

  Part of my fear is being afraid of what others will think
of me. I need to remember that it is OK to be undone in front
of others. It is important for them to see me struggle, cling to
you, and watch your power on display in my life.
I can even hold this up like a masterpiece of grace and give
you all the glory.

threadbare prayer:

LORD, your power shows up best in my weakness.

Pray without ceasing, give thanks in all circumstances;
for this is the will of God in Christ Jesus for you.

1 Thessalonians 5:17-18

Lord,

How many times I have found myself recently focusing only on the hard parts of life? My heart needs to be reminded in this season to decide ahead of time to thank Him for all things—good and hard. Both are equally part of your plan for me.

I will:
 pray constantly
  recognize your authority in my life
   decide ahead of time to be grateful

You:
 Want me to pray
  Reposition my heart when I'm thankful
   Have a purpose for my life

Thankfulness is a position of the heart and turns me towards you. When my heart is turned toward you, I am able to see things from your perspective. This is humbling but trains my eyes to see that you are here and you are working all around me.

threadbare prayer:

LORD, I will pray constantly with gratitude for all things.

*And without faith it is impossible to please him,
for whoever would draw near to God must believe that
he exists and that he rewards those who seek him.*

Hebrews 11:6

Lord,

Thank you, Lord, for what you reveal to me in your
Word. You don't hide yourself from me but invite me
to open the Bible for myself. You even promise to reward
me when I seek you.

I :
  draw near
      believe in you
          seek you

You:
  are willing to be found
      reward my faith
          reveal yourself to me

Being a student of your Word also takes discipline. I need to make a commitment to read your Word consistently. It also takes determination to pause, listen, and be still. This is how faith is grown and I become a friend of the most-high God. You are my true reward and my heart's desire.

threadbare prayer:

LORD, you are my reward when I earnestly seek you.

> *"They will make war on the Lamb, and the Lamb will conquer them, for he is Lord of lords and King of kings, and those with him are called and chosen and faithful."*
>
> Revelations 17:14

Lord,

Faith means I am called to comprehend something greater myself. I don't always understand right now, but someday I will see clearly. You are *incomprehensible* and though my heart can't really conceive of it, I will choose to believe it.

I am:
    called
        chosen
            with you in the end

You are:
    The conquering Lamb
        Lord of lords
            King of kings

I stand amazed that the sacrifice for my sins—my leader, my sovereign, my commander—invites me to be *with* Him as he delivers the final blow to my enemy. Though the end is already written, I also have the reassurance that you are leading the way, my path is marked out, and I can follow you. No matter what happens today or tomorrow, you hold my future in your hands, and you have already won.

threadbare prayer:

LORD, I know the end of the story is "You win" and I get to be with you.

And we know that the Son of God has come and has given us understanding, so that we may know him who is true; and we are in him who is true, in his Son Jesus Christ. He is the true God and eternal life. Little children, keep yourselves from idols.

1 John 5:20-21

Lord,

When I am struggling, I am tempted to run to other things to make me feel better instead of seeking you. But you desire to give me so much more than comfort, you came that I might also know you in truth.

I:
    sometimes value comfort the most
        am tempted to follow my flesh
            have a divided heart

You:
    Came to give me a mind that knows truth
        Are the true God and eternal life
            Deserve my wholehearted devotion

The easy and comfortable things I run to quickly turn into idols when I want them more than I want you. They are cheap substitutes that never satisfy the ache in my soul. You are the only one true God who deserves all of my devotion.

threadbare prayer:

LORD, I want you more than anything else.

And he who was seated on the throne said, "Behold, I am making all things new." Also he said, "Write this down, for these words are trustworthy and true."

REVELATIONS 21:5

Lord,

I need to believe that you are working right now and will continue to do so. Of course, you knew this and wrote it down as one of your final promises so I would have no doubts.

I:
    see what are doing
        hear what you say
            read what is written

You are:
    Active
        Author of the future
            Seated on the throne

You specialize in taking broken, worn out, and useless things and making them fresh, whole, and purposeful by your life-giving Spirit. The good news is that because I am part of "all things," you are making me new too! That is new hope my heart needs today.

threadbare prayer:
LORD, you are making all things new.

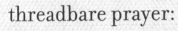

*But we have this treasure in jars of clay, to show that
the surpassing power belongs to God and not to us.
We are afflicted in every way, but not crushed; perplexed,
but not driven to despair; persecuted, but not forsaken;
struck down, but not destroyed; always carrying in
the body the death of Jesus, so that the life of Jesus may
also be manifested in our bodies. For we who live are
always being given over to death for Jesus' sake, so that
the life of Jesus also may be manifested in our mortal flesh.
So death is at work in us, but life in you.*

2 Corinthians 4:7-12

Lord,

I have come to realize that being shattered isn't the worst
thing that can happen to me. It allows other people to
plainly recognize that the source of my strength comes from
you and not from me.

I am:
> surrounded on all sides
>> not sure what to do
>>> in a low place

You:
> Go before me
>> Make a clear path
>>> Lead me to the mountaintop

While I go through what feels like is the worst, you set a boundary and say when enough is enough. In my brokennesss, I share in your suffering, die to myself, and experience your life rising up within me. If others see it too, it is worth it because they witness an extraordinary God shining in my extremely ordinary life.

threadbare prayer:

LORD, I am willing to be shattered for you to shine.

He who testifies to these things says,
"Surely I am coming soon." Amen. Come, Lord Jesus!

REVELATION 22:20

Lord,

This is why I pray. I need to be rescued from my own efforts to rule over my own little kingdom. I need to be reminded that fixing my own problems in my way will not result in peace. I need to remember I am crying out to the Alpha and the Omega who deserves not just my petitions but my praise.

I say:

Lord Jesus, come now because I am not enough.

Lord Jesus, come soon because I am weary.

Lord Jesus, come because you promised.

You say:

Surely, without a doubt

I am coming—I came and will come again

Soon, without delay

On the days when I can only whisper the word "Come" under the veil of my own tears, you still say, "Without a doubt I am coming—soon." Resolutely, I tuck myself under the shelter of your wing and hold fast to your final word. It is a promise that has been proclaimed throughout the ages that is steadfast and true.

threadbare prayer:

LORD, even so, come.

Afterward:

Who your threadbare heart needs to run to

When I was a little girl, there was no safer place for me than sitting on my daddy's lap. He would often tell me to pick out a book so he could read and sneak in some snuggle time with his only daughter. There have been so many times since his passing several years ago I have cried because I miss that sense of safekeeping. Sometimes a girl just needs her daddy to tell her everything is going to be OK. My dad's heart was tender towards me in a special way. Recently, my heavenly father showed me in a unique way that he understands my threadbare heart and longs for my questions to lead me to his very personal care and tender keeping. And he used my dad to show me.

It started that day with a 4:30 a.m. wake-up call. Fear was heavy that morning. Our family had been hit with one trial after another over the course of the past several years. On this particular morning, I felt like I was watching the domino effect of all these things hit one another and bulldoze at full force right over the top of me. It wasn't the death of my dad, my daughter's illness, my husband's cardiac arrest, unemployment, or financial stress, it was all of it at once. On this particular morning, I was lost in the mindlessness of scrolling Facebook when a video flashback started playing on my screen. It was my dad reading a passage of Scripture. The Scripture he read was:

"Therefore I tell you, do not be anxious about your life, what you will eat or what you will drink, nor about your body, what you will put on. Is not life more than food, and the body more than clothing? Look at the birds of the air: they neither sow nor reap nor gather into barns, and yet your heavenly Father feeds them. Are you not of more value than they? And which of you by being anxious can add a single hour to his span of life? And why are you anxious about clothing? Consider the lilies of the field, how they grow: they neither toil nor spin, yet I tell you, even Solomon in all his glory was not arrayed like one of these. But if God so clothes the grass of the field, which today is alive and tomorrow is thrown into the oven, will he not much more clothe you, O you of little faith? Therefore do not be anxious, saying, 'What shall we eat?' or 'What shall we drink?' or 'What shall we wear?' For the Gentiles seek after all these things, and your heavenly Father knows that you need them all. But seek first the kingdom of God and his righteousness, and all these things will be added to you. Therefore do not be anxious about tomorrow, for tomorrow will be anxious for itself. Sufficient for the day is its own trouble."

(Matthew 6:25-34)

Immediately I began sobbing into my cup of coffee. To hear my dad say the exact words I needed to hear that morning years after he had passed away was a deeply personal and moving moment for me. It was my daddy's voice telling me, "Hey, Stacey, don't worry about all those things. Your heavenly Father knows your heart. He will take care of you."

Do you know what? I'm glad my shepherd is personal like that. He knows what I need, where I'll be, and how to prepare my heart for the days ahead.

I think trials feel personal because they are; but the beauty of them being tailor-made for my heart is they lead to my shepherd who is more than able to handle every last one. It doesn't matter if you feel hurt, hidden, or hopeless. Your shepherd wants you to hear, "I know your threadbare heart. I will take care of you."

Oh friend. My prayer for you as you close this book is that you will daily take your threadbare heart to your kind, gentle, powerful, loving shepherd and let him take care of you.

Looking Forward,

Stacey